Calm your Anger

with Liam, the Smart Rabbit

Hi! I am Liam.

What is your name?

Things that Matter

Liam the rabbit lived in a deep wood.
He went to school like a smart rabbit should.
He wanted to learn and to be taught,
And dreamed of becoming an astronaut!

Usually, Liam was such a calm rabbit
With a normal, common bunny habit.
He'd munch his way through carrots galore
Then fall asleep and let out a loud snore.

One day at school something occurred:
A strange emotion inside Liam stirred.
His breathing was fast, his face turned red,
His muscles weren't relaxed but tense instead.

He looked at his paws
 and saw fists clenched,
His throat was dry
 his thirst wasn't quenched.

Liam felt like he wanted
 to cry and scream.

And from his ears?
 There was a cloud of steam!

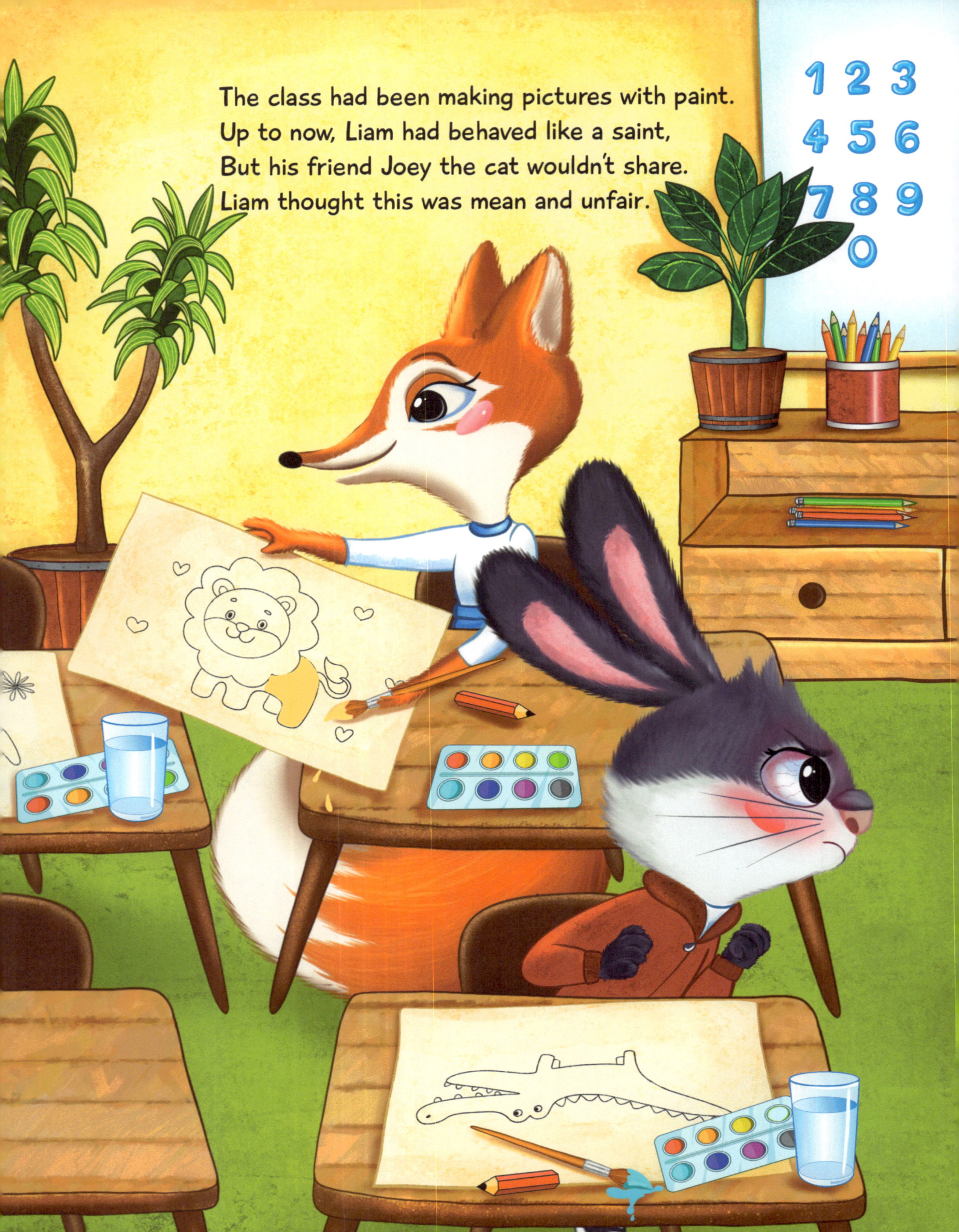

The class had been making pictures with paint.
Up to now, Liam had behaved like a saint,
But his friend Joey the cat wouldn't share.
Liam thought this was mean and unfair.

He'd coped with this for a little while,
But he needed the green paint for his crocodile!
Now all his emotions swam inside
And Liam looked angry and wide-eyed.

Mr. Raccoon said, "Liam, I see
you're getting upset.
Feelings like that, we all sometimes get.
It looks like your anger is bubbling away.
Let's try some breathing without delay.

Take a breath in and have a sniff,
A good deep breath as you get a whiff.

As you breathe in count to three:
It's as easy as saying ABC!"

Liam breathed in nice and slow
Imagining three pink roses in a row.
He felt calmer now and at ease,
His hot temper had dropped

10 degrees!

Mr. Raccoon said, "A good lesson to learn
When you feel the anger starting to burn
Is to talk your feelings through.
A friend, teacher or parent will listen to you.

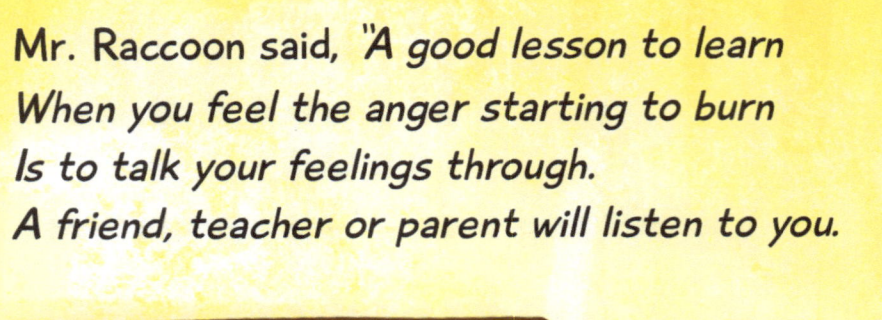

Sometimes anger is a protective mask
For strong emotion. Finding it is no simple task.

Do you actually feel

guilty, anxious, embarrassed or sad? Frustrated or fearful but hide this by feeling mad.

Try and work out what emotion you truly feel.
It's important to learn so you can then heal.
Be kind to yourself and to your feelings too,
Learn to accept yourself, as there's no one like YOU!"

"It's true!" Liam said, "Think how different it could've been.
Yes, my crocodile needed to be green.
But I could have offered a swap
Or painted it in a different color with a knitted top!"

Mr. Racoon smiled, "That's right! Congratulations!
You now all have anger calming applications.
Let's repeat today's class together
And remember the lessons forever.

First, notice when you start feeling mad.
Do some deep breathing to help you feel glad.
Ask yourself, "Why do I feel the way I feel?"
Accept the feeling, as this is how you heal.

Think about the situation from the positive side.
See what solutions can be applied.
Change the way you feel and let the anger go.
Invite calmness in and let it show."

Liam was happy that he had learned so much.
A wonderful lesson on having a calmer touch.

Perhaps you can see if this works for you too.
Why not give it a try and see how you do?

Your Opinion Matters!

If you enjoyed this book, please tell your friends about it.
Your review means a WORLD to us and will be greatly appreciated.
⭐⭐⭐⭐⭐

If the book didn't meet your expectations, please tell us
Liamthesmartrabbit@gmail.com

Learn more about Liam and download fun activities.

Copyright © 2023 by Things that Matter LLC

All rights reserved.

No part of this publication may be reproduced, distributed, or transmitted in any form or by any means, including photocopying, recording, or other electronic or mechanical methods, without the prior written permission of the publisher, except as permitted by U.S. copyright law. For permission requests, contact llcthingsthatmatter@gmail.com.

978-1-7378727-9-5 (paperback)   979-8-9880232-0-3 (hardcover)

Author Azaliya Schulz
Illustrator Daria Volkova

www.azaliyaschulz.com

Things that Matter
2023